MEL BAY

C000293929

POCKETBOOK DELUXE SERIES
by William Bay

1 2 3 4 5 6 7 8 9 0

2 **Table of Contents**

Table of Contents

3

How to Read Chord Diagrams

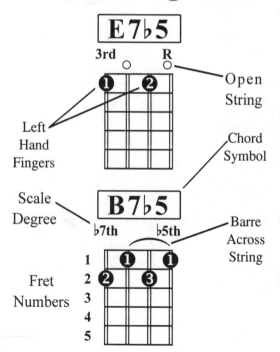

E7♭5

3rd — R

Left Hand Fingers

Open String

Chord Symbol

Scale Degree

B7♭5

♭7th — ♭5th

Barre Across String

Fret Numbers

1 2 3 4 5

Major

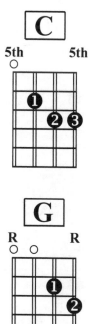

Major

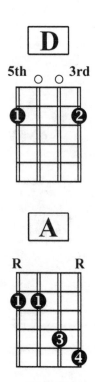

D

5th   ○   ○   3rd

A

R   R

Major

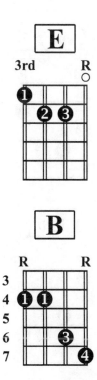

Major

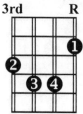

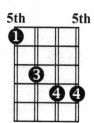

Major

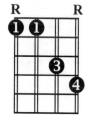

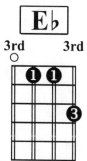

Major

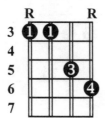

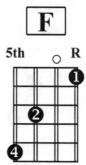

Minor

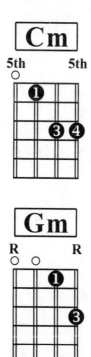

Minor

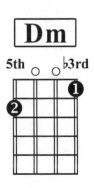

Dm

5th   ♭3rd

Am

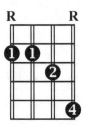

R   R

Minor

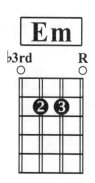

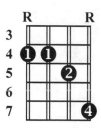

Minor

G♭m / F♯m

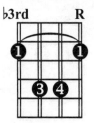

D♭m

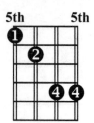

Minor

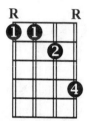

Minor

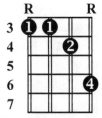

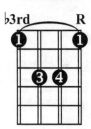

Seventh

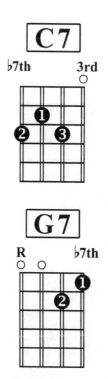

Seventh

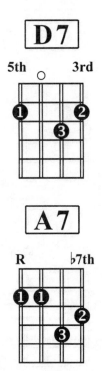

D7

5th   3rd

A7

R   ♭7th

Seventh

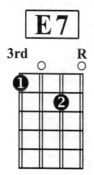

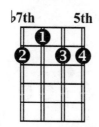

Seventh

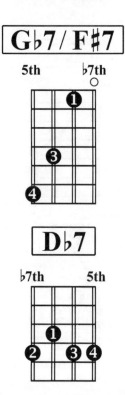

Seventh

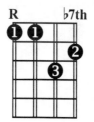

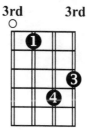

Seventh

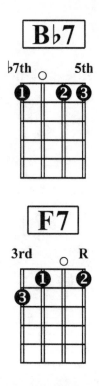

Major 7th

C Maj7

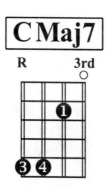

G Maj7

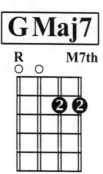

Major 7th

D Maj7

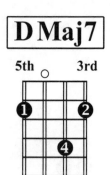

5th   ○   3rd

A Maj7

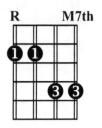

R   M7th

Major 7th

E Maj7

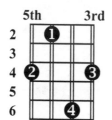

B Maj7

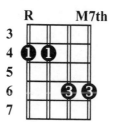

Major 7th

GbMaj7/F#Maj7

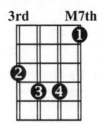

DbMaj7

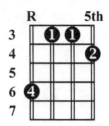

Major 7th

AbMaj7

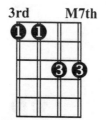

EbMaj7

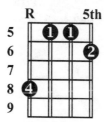

Major 7th

B♭Maj7

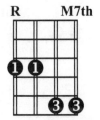

F Maj7

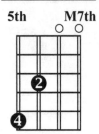

Sixth

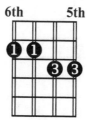

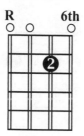

Sixth

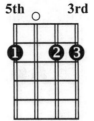

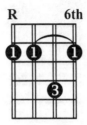

Sixth

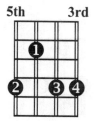

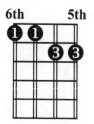

Sixth

G♭6 / F♯6

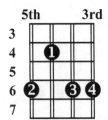

D♭6

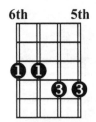

Sixth

R   6th

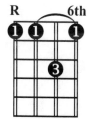

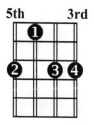

5th   3rd

Sixth

B♭6

R   6th

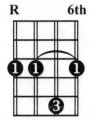

F6

5th   3rd

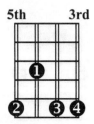

Minor 7th

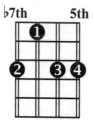

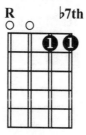

Minor 7th

Dm7

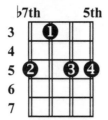

Am7

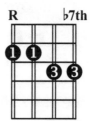

Minor 7th

Em7

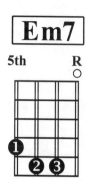

Bm7

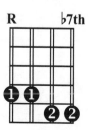

Minor 7th

G♭m7 / F♯m7

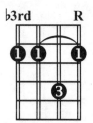

D♭m7

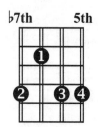

Minor 7th

A♭m7

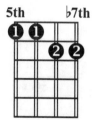

E♭m7

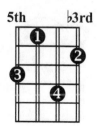

Minor 7th

B♭m7

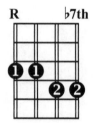

Fm7

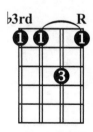

Minor 6th

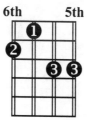

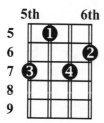

Minor 6th

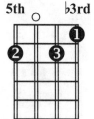

Dm6

5th   ○   ♭3rd

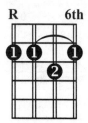

Am6

R   6th

Minor 6th

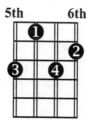

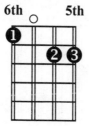

Minor 6th

G♭m6 / F♯m6

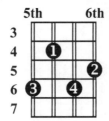

D♭m6

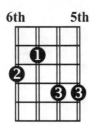

Minor 6th

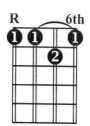

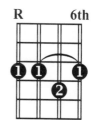

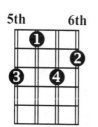

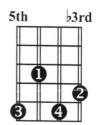

Suspended 4

Csus

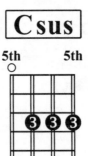

Gsus

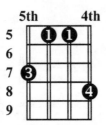

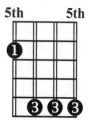

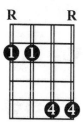

Suspended 4

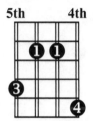

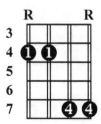

G♭sus/F♯sus

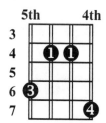

D♭sus

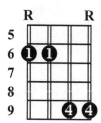

Suspended 4

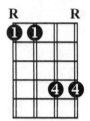

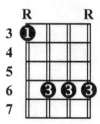

Suspended 4

B♭sus

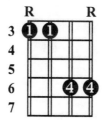

Fsus

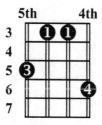

Diminished

$$B^{\circ}/D^{\circ}/F^{\circ}/A\flat^{\circ}$$

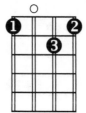

$$C^{\circ}/E\flat^{\circ}/G\flat^{\circ}/A^{\circ}$$

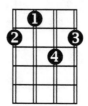

$$D\flat^\circ / E^\circ / G^\circ / B\flat^\circ$$

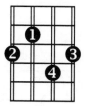

Augmented

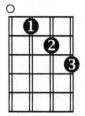

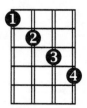

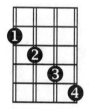

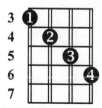

7♯5

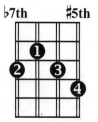

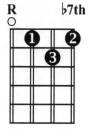

7♯5

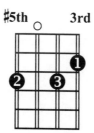

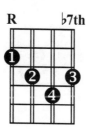

7♯5

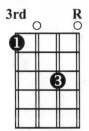

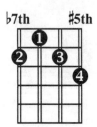

7#5

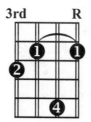

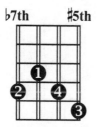

7#5

A♭7#5

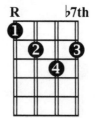

E♭7#5

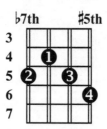

7#5

Bb7#5

♭7th   ○   #5th

F7#5

3rd   R

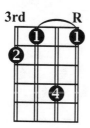

7♭5

C7♭5

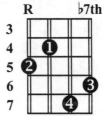

G7♭5

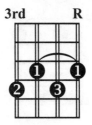

7♭5

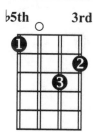

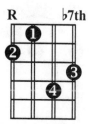

7♭5

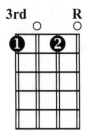

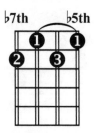

7♭5

G♭7♭5 / F♯7♭5

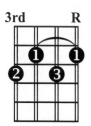

D♭7♭5

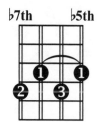

7♭5

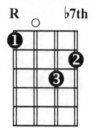

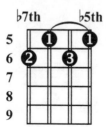

7♭5

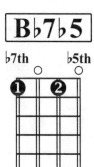

B♭7♭5

♭7th   ♭5th

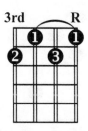

F7♭5

3rd   R

Minor7♭5

Cm7♭5

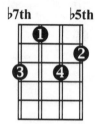

Gm7♭5

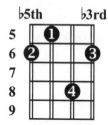

Minor7♭5

Dm7♭5

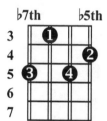

Am7♭5

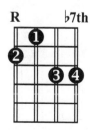

Minor7♭5

Em7♭5

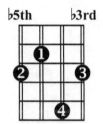

Bm7♭5

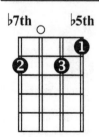

Minor7♭5

G♭m7♭5 / F♯m7♭5

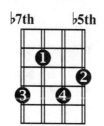

D♭m7♭5

Minor7♭5

A♭m7♭5

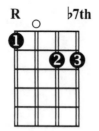

E♭m7♭5

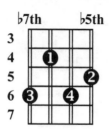

Minor7♭5

B♭m7♭5

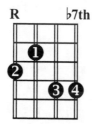

Fm7♭5

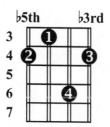

Ninth

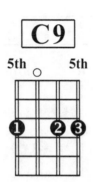

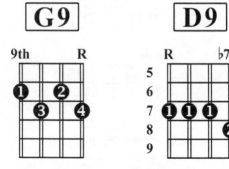

Ninth

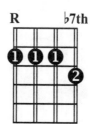

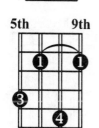

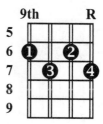

Ninth

Gb9/F#9

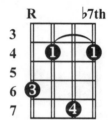

Db9

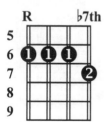

Ab9

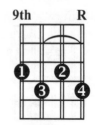

Ninth

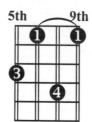

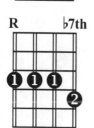

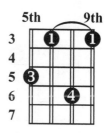

Major9th

Cma9

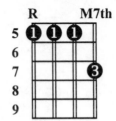

Gma9

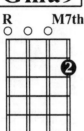

Dma9

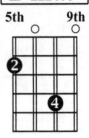

Major9th

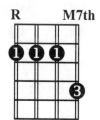

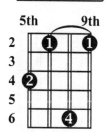

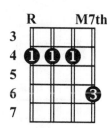

Major9th

G♭ma9/F♯ma9

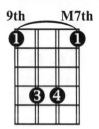

D♭ma9

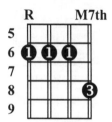

A♭ma9

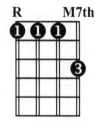

Major9th

E♭ma9

B♭ma9

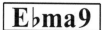

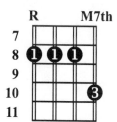

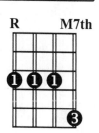

Fma9

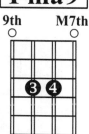

Minor9th

Cm9

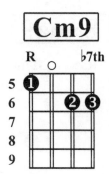

Gm9

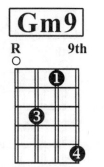

Dm9

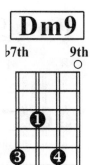

Am9

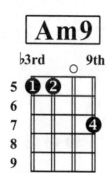

Em9

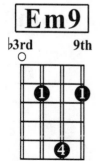

Bm9

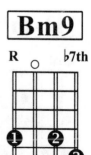

Minor9th

G♭m9 / F♯m9

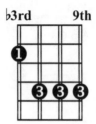

D♭m9

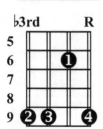

A♭m9

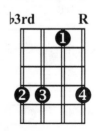

Minor9th

Ebm9

Bbm9

Fm9

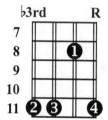

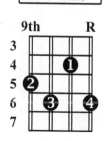

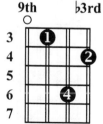

Eleventh

C11

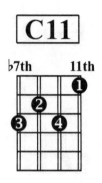

G11

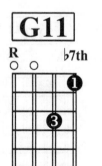

D11

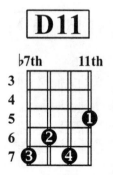

Eleventh

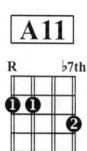

A11

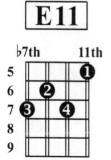

E11

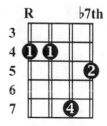

B11

Eleventh

Gb11 / F#11

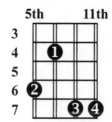

Db11

Ab11

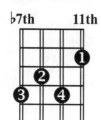

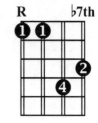

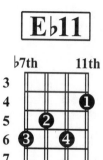

E♭11

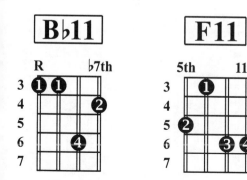

B♭11

F11

Thirteenth

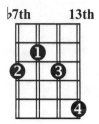

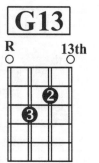

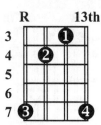

Thirteenth

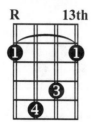

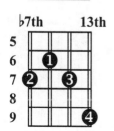

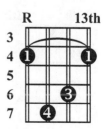

Thirteenth

Gb13/ F#13

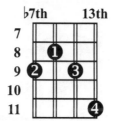

Db13

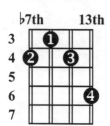

Ab13

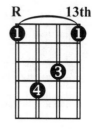

Thirteenth

Eb13

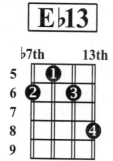

Bb13   ## F13

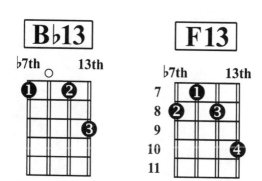

Minor13th

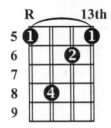

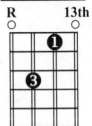

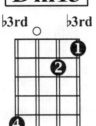

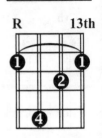

Minor13th

Em13

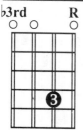

Bm13

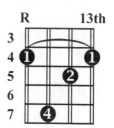

Gb/F#m13

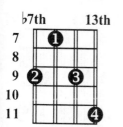

Dbm13

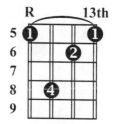

Minor13th

Abm13

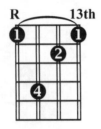

Ebm13

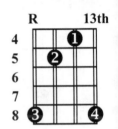

Bbm13

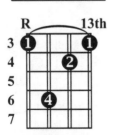

Fm13

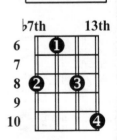